BRYCE CANYON

A SCENIC WONDERLAND

BY STEVEN L. WALKER

Front Cover: A view from Sunset Point. Bryce Canyon is not really a canyon, but is a series of amphitheaters developed by headward erosion radiating from the eastern rim of the Paunsaugunt Plateau.
PHOTO BY GARY LADD

Above: Snow covers covers the eroded formations of Bryce Canyon in this winter scene from Paria View.
PHOTO BY DICK DIETRICH

Left: The Pink Cliffs, a part of the Wasatch Formation.
PHOTO BY CHARLES CHANLEY

BRYCE CANYON...

A land of constant change, throughout each day, season, and the years, Bryce Canyon's vistas seem to change from early morning light to evening's final rays. A few short steps in any direction, a partial turn of the head, and a new perspective can be experienced from nearly every vantage point. Intricate rock formations of the Canyon have been a source of inspiration to all who have viewed them, from Indians who occupied the region more than 11,000 years ago, to the most recent visitors, the natural wonder of Bryce Canyon touches everyone in its own special way.

Among the earliest settlers, the difficulty of supporting their families in the arid lands surrounding Bryce Canyon often left little time for enjoying the scenery. Early Mormon settlers, carpenter Ebenezer Bryce and his wife Mary for whom Bryce Canyon was later named, first moved into the area around 1875 and gave it the unlikely, and less than endearing, epithet; "A hell of a place to lose a cow!"

Preceding the arrival of the Mormons and other white settlers, the Paiute Indians who populated the region referred to Bryce Canyon as "Unka-timpe-wa-wince-pock-ich", which roughly translates to "red rocks standing like men in a bowl-shaped canyon." Although Indian legends attached spiritual values to Bryce Canyon, the Paiutes, and their predecessors, used the area on occasion for hunting and gathering, finding the canyon less than bountiful, and sought greener pastures whenever possible.

In reality, Bryce Canyon is not actually a canyon at all, but is in fact an amphitheater created by forces of erosion on the more than 50 million year old rocks of the Pink Cliffs. The uppermost step in the Grand Staircase, the Pink Cliffs are part of a series of geologic layers that were uplifted and rise in a stair like fashion from the Grand Canyon in the south to Bryce Canyon in the north. With elevations reaching more than 9,100 feet on the Pink Cliffs, the Grand Staircase unfolds south to the Grey Cliffs, with deposits visible at the base of Bryce Canyon, that are more than 120 million years old.

The varied shapes of Bryce Canyon's naturally sculpted rock formations create visions of varied scenes for the observer. The rock's colors; reds and yellows the result of iron oxides in the rocks, lavenders and purples caused by the presence of manganese; are ever changing from sunrise to sunset. As the apparent light changes, it lends a brilliance to the scene that often makes certain formations seem almost transparent as they are backlit by the sun.

In stark contrast with the rugged topography of the "badlands" areas of Bryce Canyon, where erosion and steep slopes limit plant growth, the forest areas of Bryce are home to a wide variety of flora and fauna. Bryce Canyon's forests range from dwarf pinyon and juniper in the lower elevations, to spruce, aspen, and fir in higher elevations.

Right: Early morning light sets Thor's Hammer and surrounding formations aglow in this view from Sunset Point.
PHOTO BY JEFF GNASS

Below: View from Inspiration Point of Bryce Amphitheater.
PHOTO BY GARY LADD

Following Pages: Afternoon light adds beauty to Bryce Point, named for early Mormon settlers Mary and Ebenezer Bryce.
PHOTO BY BOB CLEMENZ

GEOLOGICAL FORMATION...

The Paiute Indians inhabited lands in and around Bryce Canyon for many centuries and told a story of the canyon's past where they once lived, along with many god-like animal spirits, who had the ability to appear as people. The most powerful of these spirits was Coyote, who was quite mischievous. One day Coyote stole the children of the great Water Monsters, who retaliated by flooding the region and driving the people and spirits who lived in the canyon to higher grounds.

The Paiutes, having reached their limits of tolerance for his pranks, cast Coyote from their ranks. Only the spirit lizards, toads, insects, and bats stayed in the Canyon with Coyote. In time, these spirits, grew lazy and insolent. Coyote, tiring of their behavior, called a council meeting. The spirits came in their human forms, wearing their most colorful clothing, and gathered in rows along the canyon walls. As Coyote became increasingly angrier during the council, he cast a magic spell that transformed the spirits into stone where they stood. Still today, they can be seen standing silently along the canyon's walls.

Part of the Paiute's legend is surprisingly close to the actual causes of the formation of Bryce Canyon. Water indeed played a major role in creating the region. Around 60 million years ago, during the Eocene Epoch of the Tertiary period, much of southern Utah was covered by inland seas and lakes, which deposited beds of silt, sand, and lime that reached thicknesses of up to 2,000 feet. These deposits were transformed, over the following millions of years and under great pressures, into sedimentary rock formations of multi-colored Wasatch limestone, the characteristic formation of Bryce Canyon. Waters of Lake Flagstaff, the ancient lake that covered thousands of square miles of the region, fluctuated greatly in size and shape as long term climactic shifts altered the amounts of water and sediments flowing into the area.

Left: Early morning in March finds patches of snow in Queen's Garden. Rain and snow are two of the major forces of erosion in Bryce Canyon, slicing gullies and ridges into the soft rock.
PHOTO BY JEFF GNASS

Above: The Rabbit, a formation in Agua Canyon. The harder materials composing the caprock protect the slender pillar of the formation where softer deposits have eroded away.
PHOTO BY JERRY SIEVE

Over millions of years, Lake Flagstaff received deposits of varied composition. Some were rock in solid form, and others dissolved minerals, muds, silts, and sand. Heavier rock and gravels were deposited on stream and river beds and near the lakes' constantly shifting shorelines. Lighter silts sank further from shore, while the finer clays and precipitated calcium carbonate, a natural mineral cement, settled in the deeper waters near Lake Flagstaff's center.

Around 15 million years ago, great tensions caused by the collision of the earth's plates, uplifted the entire Colorado Plateau, which covers about 150,000 square miles of Utah, Arizona, New Mexico, and Colorado. The plateau rose slowly, starting from the south, for several thousand feet, while at the same time, stress and strain broke the Colorado Plateau along north-south fractures into several plateaus, which also uplifted first from the south, causing the entire region to have a downward south-north slope. As the slope of the land increased, the gentle flowing streams and rivers that had laid the sedimentary deposits in the region were transformed into raging torrents of water and began the process of eroding away the layers of sediments and carving the steps of what geologists call the Grand Staircase. Paunsaugunt Plateau, with the Pink Cliffs of Wasatch Limestone, is the northernmost step and the site of Bryce Canyon.

Between Bryce Canyon and Zion the next step on the Grand Staircase, the Grey Cliffs, exposes deposits between 120 and 135 million years ago. Zion has the White Cliffs, which shows deposits that are up to 165 million years old. The Vermillion Cliffs, with formations between 165 million and 200 million years old, are between Zion and the Grand Canyon as are the Belted, or Chocolate, Cliffs that expose deposits formed between 200 and 225 million years ago. The Kaibab Plateau, with deposits more than 225 million years old, is the lowest step on the Grand Staircase and is part of the north rim of the Grand Canyon. The deposits of the Kaibab Plateau are the youngest found in the Grand Canyon, which exposes rock nearly two billion years old.

Right: Silent City's weathered rows of pinnacles, formed by processes of erosion and weathering greatly accelerated by jointing, resembles the remains of a lost city. Jointing caused the brittle rock of Bryce to crack, or break, vertically. Joints start as small cracks, enlarging as plant roots and frost wedging split the cracks ever further apart.
PHOTO BY JERRY JACKA

Following Pages: Heavily eroded formations of Queen's Gardens. Bryce Canyon is famous around the world for its unique erosional patterns. Bryce Canyon was given National Park status by Congress in 1928.
PHOTO BY JEFF GNASS

Below: Wall of Windows along Peekaboo Loop Trail is the result of frost-wedging, caused as water enters into rock niches, freezes and expands to enlarge the niche. Windows are formed as niches from both sides of a ridge meet to form an opening in the rock.
PHOTO BY DICK DIETRICH

Right: Ponderosa pine growing among sculpted formations near Sunset Point. As the morning light touches these formations, they appear to be almost transparent. The red and yellow colors of the pillars are the result of iron oxides in the rocks.
PHOTO BY GARY LADD

HUMAN HISTORY...

Although little archeological evidence of Paleo-Indians has been found in areas surrounding Bryce Canyon, it is commonly thought that small bands of hunters were preying on camels, horses, mammoths, and sloths in the region more than 11 thousand years ago. As large game animals disappeared, due to climactic changes and pressure from early hunters, seed gathering and small game were sought in the region by Desert Culture Indians, migratory foragers who dominated most of the southwest region from about 3,000 B.C. until the first century A.D. It is likely members of this early culture found their way to areas near Bryce Canyon, although there is little besides seed-grinding stones, split-twig figurines, and simple baskets to record their presence in areas south of Bryce Canyon.

Beginning around 700 A.D., Basketmaker Indians were inhabiting villages in Paria Valley, to the east of the Park. The Basketmakers were skilled in weaving natural fibers, making pottery, and hunting with bows and arrows. They planted crops of corn and squash as an alternative to a nomadic lifestyle of foraging.

Around 1,000 A.D., Pueblo Indians moved into areas east of the canyon where warm valleys offered land more suitable to farming than Bryce Canyon. The canyon did serve as a source of timber, food plants, and small game for the Pueblo Indians. By the 1300's, the Pueblo Indians had withdrawn from the region for reasons as yet unknown.

As the Pueblo left the region, Paiutes began to settle the Bryce Canyon area. A Peaceful, semi-nomadic people, the Paiutes were basically hunter-gatherers, although they farmed along streams and near springs using irrigation and cultivation techniques learned from earlier contact with the Pueblo. Paiutes occupied the region for several centuries, plagued by attacks from Navajos and Utes who ventured into the area searching for animal pelts and any

Left: This aerial view of Bryce Canyon gives a vantage point unseen by earlier explorers. Maze-like formations and a lack of reliable water supply discouraged human occupation
PHOTO BY GARY LADD

Above: Modern explorers tour Bryce Canyon by much the same means as earlier visitors. Horseback riding and hiking trails wind throughout most of the canyon.
PHOTO BY DICK DIETRICH

bounty they could capture in raids on Paiute settlements.

In 1776, Spanish missionaries, Fathers Escalante and Dominguez, became the first Europeans to explore southern Utah. The missionaries, in search of an overland route to connect missions in California with those in New Mexico, spent two nights in camping in the region while searching for a river crossing, but did not venture into Bryce Canyon.

In 1826, mountain man Jedediah Smith became the first American to visit the region, traveling the Old Spanish Trail. Four years later, trapper George Yount passed to the northwest of the Park enroute to California. Traders, miners, and trappers traveled the Old Spanish Trail, passing some forty miles to the north of Bryce Canyon between 1830 and 1850. No record of these groups discovering Bryce Canyon has ever been found.

Mormons first arrived in the Sevier River valley in 1852, and in 1864 settled a remote outpost at Panguitch. In the following year, Panguitch was abandoned as the Utes, Navajos, and Paiutes joined forces against the Mormon encroachment on their lands. Mormon militia, under the command of Captain James Andrus, were dispatched to fight the marauding Indians in 1866, and were probably the first white men to visit the eastern Paunsaugunt Plateau. In 1872, Major John Wesley Powell and geographer Alvin Thompson, made the first survey of Bryce Canyon and the surrounding areas. In 1874, Mormon settlers began inhabiting the upper Paria Valley. In 1875 or 1876, carpenter Ebenezer Bryce and his wife Mary, for whom the canyon was later named, moved to Clifton near the Pink Cliffs, and grazed his cattle in the lands below Sunset Point. Ebenezer Bryce assisted in early unsuccessful attempts to irrigate the Paria Valley, later leaving the area and moving to Arizona's White Mountains.

In 1905, the Paunsaugunt Plateau was declared a national forest. In 1919, Reuben Syrett built the first tourist accommodations in Bryce Canyon, the "Tourist Rest", which he later moved and renamed Rubys Inn in 1923, as Bryce Canyon became a national monument. In 1928, Congress established Bryce Canyon National Park.

Right: The brilliant gold leaves of an aspen at Fairyland Point frame a view of Sinking Ship formation in the distance. Fall represents the culmination of the life cycle of a leaf. Before the leaves fall from the tree, all valuable minerals and nutrients are transported from the leaf to avoid their loss. As soon as this process begins, the leaves stop producing chlorophyll, the substance that causes their green color, to conserve their energy and existing nutrients. As chlorophyll gradually fades away, the other pigments present in the leaf begin to show through. The yellows are xanthophyll and red and orange colors are carotene. The fall colors gain vibrance as these pigments become more visible.
PHOTO BY BOB CLEMENZ

Below: The Upper Sonoran Life Zone at Bryce Canyon National Park's north end, also referred to as the pygmy forest, includes Gambel oak, pinyon pine, Utah juniper, and red scrub oak.
PHOTO BY SUZANNE CLEMENZ

Right: The ponderosa pine's cinnamon-colored bark and green needles form a bold contrast with the delicate golden colors of aspen in fall in the park's higher elevations.
PHOTO BY BOB CLEMENZ

Above: A winter snowfall blankets the Table Cliffs in this view from Inspiration Point. Precipitation in Bryce Canyon averages 25 inches annually in the higher elevations along the plateau, much of it in the form of snowfall.
PHOTO BY JEFF GNASS

Right: Freshly fallen snow adds a mantle of white to Ponderosa pine nestled against Wasatch formations of the Pink Cliffs. The whitish color of the rocks indicate beds of limestone that have had most of their mineral content leached out.
PHOTO BY JEFF GNASS

Right: A dusting of light snowfall covers the landscape shortly after the passing of a winter storm in this view from Bryce Point. Water from melting snow seeps into the cracks and joints of rocks. As it freezes as nighttime temperatures fall, its volume expands about ten percent and exerts around two thousand pounds of pressure per square inch, prying the rock into angular fragments in a process called frost-wedging.
PHOTO BY BOB CLEMENZ

Following Pages: Blue skies and sunshine illuminate formations covered by pure white snows in this view from Sunset Point.
PHOTO BY DICK DIETRICH

THE BADLANDS...

Although the term "Badlands" may conjure images of lands unsuitable for human inhabitation, at Bryce Canyon the name came about quite innocently enough. Eighteenth century French fur trappers termed lands that were difficult to traverse as "les mauvaises terres à traverser", which meant the bad lands to cross. The phrase, shortened by American explorers, traders, and trappers, ultimately became simply "the badlands". Natural geological features of Bryce Canyon, its sheer walls and steep slopes, fin-like ridges, box canyons, jagged columns, and pinnacles make attempts to traverse the canyon an arduous task.

Summer temperatures often become stifling, and the high altitude, between 8,000 and 9,000 feet, can make journeys across the badlands a trial for most. Although most of the park remains open throughout winter, except during and shortly after snowstorms, winter treks can be nearly impossible for anyone not experienced with snowshoes or cross country skiing.

The badlands has often been a term used to describe lands difficult to cross, or that are inhospitable. Bryce Canyon and Cedar Breaks, a smaller canyon west of Bryce Canyon, are unique among badlands of the world. Formations at Bryce Canyon are a result of effects of erosion, weathering, climate, on the composition of rock found in the area. The resulting formations have created a landscape that has fascinated visitors from around the world for nearly a century.

The sculptured pinnacles and fanciful formations found in Bryce Canyon are characterized by patterns of horizontal bedding planes and vertical cracks, or joints, which are a major factor in determining the basic structures of the badlands. The physical process that shapes the fanciful spires, windows, and ridges of the canyon are directly

Above: The Hunter in Agua Canyon. Plants seen growing on the top of the formation will add to its final end by a process called organic weathering in which roots pry the rock apart.
PHOTO BY JERRY SIEVE

Left: Rows of rock towers catch the afternoon light below Bryce Point. The badlands of Bryce Canyon were created as forces of erosion carved intricate formations from sedimentary deposits laid by the ancient Lake Flagstaff around 60 million years ago.
PHOTO BY BOB CLEMENZ

linked to processes that decompose, or erode, the rock. Erosion from running water, chemical weathering, frost wedging, granular disintegration, organic elements, and weathering all contribute to the continuing erosion that shapes the canyon's badlands.

Streams and running water, formed by rain and melting snow, are responsible for down-cutting which carves the rocks based on the degree of hardness the rock formations possess. The more resistant limestone formations erode at slower rates than softer shale or sandstone, forming shelves, caprocks, and ledges that protect remnants of their bases. Deeper amphitheaters of the park were carved by the most active intermittent streams. The canyon's walls on the eastern edge of the Paunsaugunt Plateau are still receding to the northwest at a rate of approximately a foot every fifty years.

Chemical weathering is caused as mineral laden solutions penetrate into rock from cracks and crevices and add to the overall process of erosion by breaking rock into pieces easily removable by running water. Solutions of seeping water penetrate weak layers of rock and dissolve the calcium-carbonate cement that binds the individual grains, turning rock into sand.

Granular disintegration is caused by freezing and thawing, a process that can occur as many as 200 times a year, and extremes of temperature that cause mineral grains to separate, forming coarse sands or gravel. Frost wedging forces rock apart as water seeps into the rock, freezes, expands its volume, and exerts tremendous pressure to pry the rock apart. Organic weathering is caused as roots of plants and trees pry rock apart, animals burrow holes, or human endeavors cause the removal of material.

The badlands of Bryce Canyon are the direct result of the ongoing forces of erosion and are constantly changing their features. Bryce Canyon's badlands should be seen as ever changing sculptures. Areas that today are sheer canyon walls will in the future undoubtedly be transformed into arches, bridges, pinnacles, fin-ridges, windows, and spires, ever replacing older features removed by erosion.

Right: The Two Bridges in Bryce Canyon National Park. Bridges, windows, arches, and other oddly shaped formations are examples of differential erosion, weathering, and seeping groundwater on the rock of the Wasatch Formation. As the ancient Lake Flagstaff laid its deposits of sediments over a period of millions of years, they varied in degree of hardness. As the underlying deposits of softer sediments are subjected to forces of erosion, they often leave layers of harder deposits to form bridges, arches, or cap rocks.
PHOTO BY STEVE BRUNO

Below: Pine boughs frame Queen Victoria. A resemblance to the Queen still remains although photographs show extensive erosion of the Queen's crown has occurred in the past thirty years.
PHOTO BY JEFF GNASS

Right: Pinnacles and Ponderosa pine in Fairyland Canyon. The snow visible in the background adds to a freeze-thaw process that occurs more than 200 times a year in Bryce Canyon.
PHOTO BY JERRY SIEVE

THE FORESTED PLATEAU...

The forests of Bryce Canyon National Park offer a striking contrast to the highly eroded formations of the canyon. Three vegetative zones, or plant communities, are found in the park; the Upper Sonoran, Transition, and Canadian. Although there are no hard boundaries between the different zones, and species will occasionally intermingle as slope exposure, the direction a slope faces, changes the life zones normal limits, each of these habitats generally supports their own diversity of flora and fauna that have adapted to conditions and challenges of life found within the individual zones.

The Upper Sonoran Life Zone occurs in areas below 7,000 feet in elevation and is home to the pinyon-Juniper, or pygmy, forests which are normally found below the canyon's rim. With an annual precipitation of only 13 inches, and summer temperatures that often exceed a hundred degrees followed by winter temperatures that can fall to 20 degrees below zero, only hardy species of trees and plants are able to survive.

Pinyon pine, Utah juniper, and sagebrush are the most predominant plant species and share the Upper Sonoran Life Zone with Gambel oak, manzanita, cliffrose, and a variety of flowering plants able to survive temperature extremes and the extended periods of droughts.

The Transition Zone is home to the ponderosa pine forests found in elevations between 7,000 and 8,500 feet. With increased moisture from rainfall and snow melt, averaging between 18 and 20 inches per year, the Transition Zone supports a greater variety of flora and fauna than in the other life zones. Here, taller trees, more luxuriant shrubs, and much of the wildlife found in the region can be found. Ponderosa pine form stately stands with specimens reaching as much as five hundred years old. Green-leaf manzanita grows along the rim and beneath the ponderosa pine along with bitterbrush, snowberry, aspen, elderberry,

Above: Bryce Canyon National Park is home to ponderosa pine, which grow to heights of more than one hundred feet and are found in the Transition Life Zone.
PHOTO BY DICK DIETRICH

mountain mahogany, and Oregon grape. The shrubs and seedlings are a favorite food of browsing animals and the berry crops are an important part of the food chain for a variety of birds and animals.

The ponderosa pine forest is thought to have been the most frequented area in the park by earlier inhabitants who relied on seeds, grains, game, and berries found in the forest for food. The ponderosa pine forest was also used as an important source of raw materials for medicines, dyes, and building materials. The native inhabitants were able to harvest the bounty of the forest without causing their destruction, unlike the Anglo pioneers who decimated large tracts of land when cutting trees for lumber and over grazed meadows for use as summer pastures.

The Canadian Life Zone has the highest elevations found in the park and are home to the spruce-fir-aspen forest, which is found in elevations about 9,000 feet. Douglas fir, aspen, blue spruce, and white fir form dense stands, while bristlecone and limber pine are found in exposed areas of the high plateau.

The Canadian Zone offers harsh conditions for survival of plant species. Low winter temperatures, heavy snowfall, and high winds damage the trees and high altitude winds and sun cause dehydration in summer. Canadian Zone trees must complete their annual growth cycle before being exposed to late or early frosts.

White fir and Douglas fir grow to more than 100 feet tall but have shallow roots and are endangered by high winds, disease, and insect populations. The twisted bristlecone and limber pine are perhaps the only tree species suited to more exposed areas of the Canadian Life Zone. Limber pine have extremely flexible branches and are able to survive high winds and withstand heavy loads of snow and ice. Bristlecone, with the ability to survive under the harshest conditions, are the oldest living organisms on earth. Parts of the tree remain alive while other parts die, and the tree rebounds when conditions for growth improve. Bristlecone reach ages of around 5,000 years, with the oldest specimens in Bryce Canyon thought to be about 1,700 years old.

Left: Bryce Canyon National Park, with altitudes ranging from 6,600 to 9,100 feet, features three distinct forest types, Juniper and pinyon pine, ponderosa pine (shown here), and spruce-aspen-fir.
PHOTO BY CHARLES CHANLEY

BRYCE CANYON WILDLIFE...

Bryce Canyon National Park's three life zones support a diverse variety of wildlife. In the lower elevations of the pinyon-juniper forest found in the Upper Sonoran Life Zone, pinyon nuts and juniper berries provide food for deer mice, the least and cliff chipmunks, wood rats, and pinyon jays, which in turn become prey for predators including the grey fox, bobcats, coyotes, and ringtail cats. Insects provide a rich food source for mountain bluebirds, white-breasted nuthatches, northern flickers, along with other bird species and also for a reptile population including gopher snakes, garter snakes, sagebrush lizards, skinks, short-horned lizards, and the poisonous Great Basin rattlesnakes.

The ponderosa pine forest of the Transition Life Zone is the habitat populated by most of the animal and bird species found in the park. The seeds, nuts, berries, and vegetation of the Transition Zone feeds a large population of rodents including the golden-mantled ground squirrels, pine squirrels, Uinta chipmunks, white-tailed prairie dogs, marmots, jack-rabbits, and cottontail rabbits. These smaller mammals are in turn prey for badgers, skunks, weasels, gray fox, coyotes, bobcats, and ring-tailed cats along with the much larger and more elusive cougar, also called puma or mountain lion, which preys primarily on the park's more than abundant population of mule deer.

Mule deer are the largest of the mammals found in the park

Above: The great horned owl is carnivorous, feeding on small mammals, including rabbits and rodents, and other birds. The owls makes their nests in trees and in the cliffs of the canyon.
PHOTO BY LEONARD LEE RUE III

and can be encountered at times throughout each of Bryce Canyon's life zones. The mule deer browse on shrubs and seedlings to keep the forest in check and maintain meadows. The rugged terrain below the Pink Cliffs of Bryce Canyon is one of the few remaining refuge areas in western North America for the mountain lions, whose numbers have been drastically reduced by humans in recent years through excessive hunting and trapping. The cougars have formed a mutually beneficial predator-prey relationship with the mule deer. An individual cougar may kill as many as fifty mule deer each year, culling the weaker members of the herd by taking the old, young, or sick animals, and thus helping to preserve a healthy and balanced deer population. Reducing the overall size of the mule deer population assures that the remaining members will not be decimated by starvation resulting from their own over browsing, which will occur when their numbers are left unchecked.

Porcupines are one of the most unusual creatures to be found in the ponderosa pine forests. Their sharp quills act as a deadly deterrent to most predators who chose to leave the porcupine alone to feed on wildflowers, berries, bark, leaves, nuts, and even young ponderosa pine and other trees when the winter snows are particularly heavy.

Most species frequent the spruce-fir-aspen forests of the Canadian Zone only in summer months, preferring warmer climates of the lower elevations to more intense winters found in the higher country. Mule deer are often seen here in the summer, along with small populations of black bear, cougar, and elk. The park was once home to bighorn sheep, grizzly bears, beavers, and timber wolves, all of which have been eliminated by man.

During October, as winter weather approaches, most of the species found in the Canadian Zone begin their migrations to lower elevations. The larger mammals, including the deer, cougar, and elk, head for warmer climates while many of the small mammals dig in to prepare for winter, ground squirrels and marmots hibernating until the warmer weather of spring return.

Bryce Canyon National Park provides habitat for more than 164 species of birds, including red-tailed hawks, woodpeckers, great horned owls, ravens, flycatchers, swallows, jays, chickadees, wrens, thrushes, nuthatches, blue grouse, sparrows and many more. Most species, with the notable exception of hawks, owls, nuthatches, ravens, blue grouse, and jays, remain in the park from spring to fall, migrating to warmer climates as winter nears.

Left: Mule deer are commonly found grazing on the plateaus.
PHOTO BY MIKE SCULLY
Preceding Pages: Early summer morning scene from Paria View.
PHOTO BY STEVE BRUNO

Right: Trees of Bryce Canyon often find growing conditions harsh due to a lack of moisture and adequate soils. Trees are usually spaced far apart because of the competition for the available supply of moisture and nutrients. Roots are often exposed as the trees use their shallow roots systems to trap water during rains. The widespread root systems help to reduce erosion and act to bind the small amounts of soil available. It is not unusual to find pinyon pine and juniper appearing to grow from solid rock as their roots seek small deposits of soils found in the cracks and crevices of rocks.
PHOTO BY DICK DIETRICH

Below: The Natural Bridge is not actually a bridge but is an arch that is 95 feet tall and 54 feet wide created by weathering as the softer deposits beneath the formation were eroded away, leaving the more resistant top layers in place.
PHOTO BY DICK DIETRICH

Right: One of several washes draining Bryce Amphitheater. As summer storms deliver onslaughts of rain, a lack of vegetation on the Canyon's slopes, coupled with non-porous surfaces of the slopes, prevent rainwater from penetration and retention.
PHOTO BY STEVE BRUNO

Right: A pinyon pine frames the trailhead of the Navajo Trail at Sunset Point. Bryce Canyon National Park, created by Congress in 1928, today encompasses around 36,000 acres of intricately eroded rock formations, forests, and mountain meadows.
PHOTO BY BOB CLEMENZ

Back Cover: Departing snow clouds leave their white residue on the formations of Bryce Canyon. The Winter snows account for a large percentage of the area's annual precipitation and add significantly to the forces of erosion constantly shaping the canyon.
PHOTO BY BOB CLEMENZ

For additional copies please contact Canyonlands Publications, 4999 East Empire, Unit A, Flagstaff, Arizona 86004 or call toll free 1-800-283-1983. In this same series, Grand Canyon-Scenic Wonderland is now available, Zion National Park-Scenic Wonderland available Spring 1993. For a more in-depth natural history study of the Southwest, order Arizona-The Grand Canyon State (80 pages plus cover), or Grand Canyon-A Natural Wonder of the World (64 pages plus cover).